10 KEYS

To Successful Money Management

CHERLENE ADEWUNMI

Copyright 2023 by Cherlene Adewunmi and CAE Publications - All rights reserved. It is illegal to reproduce, duplicate, or transmit any part of this document in either electronic means or printed format. Recording of this publication is prohibited

Contents

Introduction 1

Budget Your Time 5

Write A Personal Vision for Yourself 10

Adopt A Corporate Vision for Your Family 16

Operate In Your Gifts And Talents And Increase Your Skill Set 20

Educate Yourself on Money and Credit, Take Budgeting and Financial Classes 25

Utilize A Budget For Everything Everything Has A Budget 29

Establish And Stay On Top Of Your Credit Score 38

Purchase Real Estate 41

Establish Multiple Streams of Income 45

Hold Everyone Accountable For Their Own Financial Success 49

Build Wealth for The Long Term 55

Introduction

10 Keys to Successful $ Management is a groundbreaking tool designed to empower individuals with the knowledge and skills necessary to take control other financial future. This meticulously crafted guide offers practical strategies and invaluable insights, equipping readers with the tools they need to navigate the complexities of wealth management. Each Wisdom Key provides clear, concise information that is both accessible and applicable to individuals of all financial backgrounds.

In the ancient city of Salem, lived a man named Melchizedek. Biblically, he is a mysterious figure, often referred to as the King of Salem and the High Priest of God. Melchizedek was known for his immense wealth and wisdom, which made him a respected and revered figure among the people.

One day, news reached Melchizedek's about a man named Abraham, who had recently emerged as a prominent figure in the region. Abraham was a righteous man, chosen by God to be the father of a great nation. Intrigued by this man's reputation, Melchizedek decided to meet him.

When Melchizedek and Abraham finally met, they engaged in a deep conversation about faith, blessings, and the power of God. Melchizedek recognized the divine favor upon Abraham and acknowledged him as a chosen vessel of God's plan. In a gesture of respect and honor, Melchizedek blessed Abraham and offered him bread and wine, symbolizing their newfound friendship and spiritual connection.

Abraham, deeply moved by Melchizedek's wisdom and generosity, felt compelled to show God gratitude. In an act of reverence and obedience, Abraham give a tenth of all his possessions to Melchizedek. This act of giving a tenth of one's earnings, known as a tithe, was a way for Abraham to acknowledge Melchizedek's spiritual authority and to honor God's blessings upon his own life.

The reason behind Abraham's decision to tithe to Melchizedek lies in the significance of Melchizedek's role as both a king and a priest. In the biblical account, Melchizedek is described as having no genealogy, no beginning or end, and being without father or mother. This portrayal suggests that Melchizedek was a unique and divine figure, representing God.

Abraham, being a man of faith, recognized the spiritual authority and wisdom that Melchizedek possessed. By offering a tithe, Abraham acknowledged that Melchizedek's blessings and teachings were a direct result of his connection to God. It was a way for Abraham to demonstrate his trust in God's plan and to honor the spiritual guidance he received through Melchizedek.

The act of tithing to Melchizedek also symbolized Abraham's willingness to submit to God's authority and to recognize that all blessings and wealth ultimately come from God. It was a way for Abraham to express his gratitude and to demonstrate his understanding that he was merely a steward of the resources entrusted to him.

In return for Abraham's act of faith and obedience, Melchizedek continued to bless him and prophesied about the future greatness of his descendants. This encounter between Melchizedek and Abraham became a significant moment in biblical history, highlighting the importance of faith, obedience, and the acknowledgment of God's plans for humanity.

As time went on, the story of Melchizedek and Abraham's encounter became a powerful example for future generations. It served as a reminder that wealth and blessings should be used to honor God and to support His work on earth. The act of tithing, inspired by Abraham's example, became a spiritual practice that symbolized trust, gratitude, and the acknowledgment of God's provision.

And so, the story of Melchizedek and Abraham's meeting, their exchange of blessings, and the act of tithing became a timeless lesson for humanity, reminding us of the importance of recognizing and honoring God's authority and blessings in our lives.

Budget Your Time

Embracing the notion of always operating by a budget is a fundamental principle that extends far beyond financial matters. It is a mindset, a way of life that permeates into the very fibers of our everyday existence. Time, just like money, is a precious resource that must be budgeted; otherwise, it is wasted. By setting a daily, weekly, monthly, and yearly agenda, we can effectively allocate our time, ensuring it is spent wisely and purposefully. In the world of business, a budget is not a luxury but a necessity.

Without it, a business would inevitably face financial turmoil and, ultimately, shut down. Similarly, if one aspires to manage the business of others, the ability to budget becomes a prerequisite. Business management demands a keen understanding of resource allocation and financial planning. In essence, we must learn to budget everything, starting with our time, as time, quite simply, is money. To truly excel in our professional endeavors, we must master the art of managing time effectively and efficiently.

To optimize the productivity of your time, it is important to comprehend and implement these ten wisdom keys.

1. Set clear goals: Define your short-term and long-term goals, both personal and professional. This will help you prioritize your time effectively.

2. Prioritize tasks: Identify the most important tasks that align with your goals and complete them first. This will prevent you from getting overwhelmed and ensure that you focus on what truly matters.

3. Create a schedule: Plan your days, weeks, and months in advance. Allocate specific time slots for different activities, including work, family, hobbies, and self-care. Stick to your schedule as much as possible.

4. Eliminate distractions: Minimize unnecessary distractions like social media notifications or excessive TV watching. Consider using productivity apps or website blockers to stay focused on your tasks.

5. Delegate and outsource: Identify tasks that can be delegated to others or outsourced. This will free up your time to focus on more important or enjoyable activities.

6. Practice time blocking: Allocate specific blocks of time for specific tasks. For example, dedicate a block of time each day for email management or a specific project. This helps you avoid multitasking and increases productivity.

7. .Learn to say no: Don't be afraid to say no to commitments or requests that don't align with your priorities. This allows you to protect your time and focus on what truly matters to you.

8. .Take breaks: Allow yourself regular breaks throughout the day to recharge and avoid burnout. Short breaks can actually enhance productivity by refreshing your mind.

9. .Evaluate and adjust: Regularly review your schedule and evaluate how well you're managing your time. Identify any areas where you might be wasting time or not maximizing productivity and make adjustments accordingly.

10. Practice self-care: Make sure to include time for self-care activities like exercise, relaxation, hobbies, and spending time with loved ones. Taking care of yourself will improve your overall well-being and enhance your ability to manage your time effectively.

Ecclesiastes 3:1-2 - "For everything there is a season, and a time for every matter under heaven: a time to be born, and a time to die; a time to plant, and a time to pluck up what is planted."

Psalm 90:12 - "So teach us to number our days that we may get a heart of wisdom."

Ephesians 5:15-16 - "Look carefully then how you walk, not as unwise but as wise, making the best use of the time, because the days are evil."

Colossians 4:5 - "Walk in wisdom toward outsiders, making the best use of the time."

Proverbs 20:4 - "The sluggard does not plow in the autumn; he will seek at harvest and have nothing."

James 4:14 - "Yet you do not know what tomorrow will bring. What is your life? For you are a mist that appears for a little time and then vanishes."

Galatians 6:9 - "And let us not grow weary of doing good, for in due season we will reap, if we do not give up."

Psalm 39:4-5 - "O Lord, make me know my end and what is the measure of my days; let me know how fleeting I am! Behold, you have made my days a few handbreadths, and my lifetime is as nothing before you. Surely all mankind stands as a mere breath!"

Matthew 6:34 - "Therefore do not be anxious about tomorrow, for tomorrow will be anxious for itself. Sufficient for the day is its own trouble."

Isaiah 55:6 - "Seek the Lord while he may be found; call upon him while he is near."

Write A Personal Vision for Yourself

As I reflect upon my journey and aspirations, I recognize the significance of crafting a personal vision for myself. It serves as a guiding light, directing my efforts and actions towards the attainment of my ultimate goals. With meticulous introspection and a keen understanding of my values, strengths, and aspirations, I envision a future where I am a respected leader in my chosen field, making a positive and lasting impact on the lives of others. I strive to continuously grow and develop both personally and professionally, pushing the boundaries of my potential and embracing challenges as opportunities for growth. By embracing a mindset of continuous learning, cultivating strong relationships, and embodying unwavering integrity, I aim to create a legacy that inspires and empowers those around me.

Create a Personal Development Plan and set a timeframe for achieving it.

Ex: Achieving My Personal Vision in Two Months In order to achieve our personal vision, we must have a well-defined plan that outlines the necessary steps and actions required. This personal development plan aims to guide you towards realizing your personal vision within a timeframe of two months. By following this plan diligently, you will be able to make significant progress towards your goals and create a positive impact on your life.

Step 1: Define Your Personal Vision

Take some time to reflect on your personal vision and what you want to achieve in the next two months. Write down your goals, aspirations, and the specific outcomes you desire. Be clear and specific about what you want to accomplish, as this will serve as the foundation for your plan.

Step 2: Set SMART Goals

Based on your personal vision, set SMART (Specific, Measurable, Achievable, Relevant, Time-bound) goals. Break down your vision into smaller, actionable steps that can be accomplished within the 2-month timeframe. Ensure that your goals are realistic and aligned with your personal values.

Step 3: Create an Action Plan

Now that you have defined your goals, create a detailed action plan outlining the specific tasks and activities required to achieve each goal. Prioritize your tasks based on their importance and urgency. Set deadlines for each task to maintain focus and accountability.

Step 4: Develop New Skills

Identify the skills and knowledge you need to acquire or improve upon to achieve your goals. Create a learning plan that includes reading books, attending workshops, taking online courses, or seeking mentorship. Allocate time each week to develop these skills and track your progress.

Step 5: Build a Support System

Surround yourself with individuals who support and encourage your personal growth. Seek out mentors, join relevant communities or groups, and engage in networking opportunities. Collaborate with like-minded individuals who can provide guidance, feedback, and motivation throughout your journey.

Step 6: Practice Self-Care

To maintain focus and productivity, it is crucial to prioritize self-care. Incorporate activities such as exercise, meditation, journaling, and adequate rest into your daily routine. Take care of your physical, mental, and emotional well-being to ensure sustained progress towards your goals.

Step 7: Monitor and Evaluate Progress Regularly review your progress against the goals and milestones you have set. Assess what is working well and what needs adjustment. Celebrate your achievements along the way and make necessary modifications to your plan if required. Stay adaptable and open to change.

Step 8: Stay Motivated and Persistent Maintaining motivation and persistence is key to achieving your personal vision. Remind yourself of your why and the positive impact achieving your goals will have on your life. Surround yourself with positive affirmations, visualize your success, and stay committed to your plan even during challenging times.

Conclusion:

By following this personal development plan diligently, you will be well on your way to achieving your personal vision within the next 2 months. Remember, success is a journey, and it requires consistent effort, dedication, and self- belief. Stays focused, stay motivated, and embraces the growth and transformation that comes with pursuing your personal vision.

Proverbs 29:18 - "Where there is no vision, the people perish."

Habakkuk 2:2-3 - "Write the vision; make it plain on tablets, so he may run who reads it. For still the vision awaits its appointed time; it hastens to the end it will not lie. If it seems slow, wait for it; it will surely come; it will not delay."

Jeremiah 29:11 - "For I know the plans I have for you, declares the Lord, plans for welfare and not for evil, to give you a future and a hope."

Proverbs 16:9 - The heart of man plans his way, but the Lord establishes his steps."

Ephesians 3:20 - Now to him who is able to do far more abundantly than all that we ask or think, according to the power at work within us."

Proverbs 3:5-6 - "Trust in the Lord with all your heart, and do not lean on your own understanding. In all your ways acknowledge him, and he will make straight your paths." Psalm 37:4 - "Delight yourself in the Lord, and he will give you the desires of your heart."

Isaiah 40:31 - But they who wait for the Lord shall renew their strength; they shall mount up with wings like eagles; they shall run and not be weary; they shall walk and not faint."

Philippians 3:13-14 - "Brothers, I do not consider that I have made it my own. But one thing I do: forgetting what lies behind and straining forward to what lies ahead, I *press on toward the goal for the prize of the upward call of God in Christ Jesus."*

Psalm 119:105 - "Your word is a lamp to my feet and a light to my path."

Adopt A Corporate Vision for Your Family

In order to establish a solid foundation for success and cohesion within a family unit, you should craft and embrace a corporate vision. Similar to how organizations develop mission statements to guide their actions and future endeavors, families too can greatly benefit from a clearly defined sense of purpose and direction. By creating a corporate vision for the family, individuals can align their personal aspirations with the collective goals of the household, fostering an environment of unity and shared values. Having a personal vision for one's own life, alongside the adoption of a corporate vision for the family, enables the harmonization of individual ambitions with the broader objectives of the household. This strategic approach not only instills a sense of purpose and direction, but also cultivates a collective mindset that promotes growth, resilience, and the fulfillment of both personal and familial aspirations.

Having a shared vision for your family serves as the guiding light, bringing clarity and purpose to the collective journey. When all individuals in the family operate by this vision, it creates a harmonious and thriving environment where everyone feels valued and understood. A shared vision helps build strong relationships, fosters open communication, and encourages collaboration. It allows each family member to contribute their unique strengths and talents towards a common goal, ultimately creating a sense of unity and togetherness. Moreover, having a vision promotes growth and personal development, as it sets clear expectations and provides a framework for decision-making. Embracing a shared vision for your family not only strengthens the bond among its members but also paves the way for a brighter and more fulfilling future together.

Here is a checklist to help you establish a shared vision for your family:

1. .Set aside dedicated time: Schedule a family meeting or retreat to discuss and create the corporate vision. Ensure that everyone can participate without distractions.

2. .Communicate the purpose: Explain to your family members the importance of establishing a shared

vision. Emphasize that it is about setting collective goals and working together for the benefit of all.

3. .Define values and principles: Start by identifying the core values and principles that your family holds dear. These can range from integrity and respect to entrepreneurship and philanthropy. Encourage each family member to contribute their ideas.

4. Discuss long-term goals: Encourage each family member to express their aspirations and goals for the future. These can include personal, professional, educational, and financial objectives. Ensure that everyone has an opportunity to share their thoughts.

5. Identify common interests: Look for areas where family members have shared interests or passions. These can be used as building blocks for the corporate vision, enabling everyone to contribute their talents and expertise.

6. Encourage open dialogue: Foster an environment where everyone feels comfortable expressing their opinions and concerns. Active listening and respecting differing viewpoints can lead to a more inclusive and robust vision.

7. Seek consensus: Work towards finding common ground and building consensus among family members.

Encourage compromise and collaboration to ensure that the vision reflects the collective desires of the family.

8. Draft the vision statement: Based on the discussions and consensus, develop a concise and inspiring vision statement that encapsulates the collective goals, values, and aspirations of the family. Ensure that it is clear, concise, and easy to understand.

9. Share and refine: Share the draft vision statement with all family members and invite feedback. Encourage suggestions for improvement and refine the statement until it accurately represents the collective vision.

10. Commitment and accountability: Once the final vision statement is agreed upon, emphasize the importance of commitment and accountability from all family members. Encourage everyone to actively work towards the vision and hold each other accountable.

11. Regularly review and update: Set a regular review schedule to assess progress, revise goals if necessary, and ensure that the vision remains relevant to changing circumstances. This will help keep the family engaged and motivated.

Operate In Your Gifts And Talents And Increase Your Skill Set

Operating your gifts and talents and continuously increasing your skill set is paramount in today's competitive professional landscape. As individuals, we possess unique abilities and innate talents that, when nurtured and developed, can greatly contribute to our success and fulfillment. By identifying and embracing these gifts, we not only enhance our personal effectiveness but also enrich the organizations we serve. Furthermore, actively seeking opportunities to expand our skill set allows us to adapt to ever-evolving industry trends and challenges, ensuring our relevance and marketability. By harnessing our inherent strengths and continuously honing our abilities, we position ourselves for growth, advancement, and a meaningful impact in our chosen field.

Recognizing one's gifts and talents is a crucial aspect of personal and professional growth. Understanding and leveraging these unique capabilities can lead to increased self-confidence, professional satisfaction, and overall success. One effective way to identify these gifts and talents is through self-reflection. Take time to assess your strengths and areas where you excel, paying attention to activities that bring you joy and energize you. Additionally, seeking feedback from trusted colleagues, mentors, or supervisors can provide valuable insights into your talents. Engaging in continuous learning and exploration of various domains can also uncover hidden abilities. By remaining open-minded, self-aware, and committed to self-improvement, one can successfully recognize and harness their gifts and talents, ultimately realizing their full potential in their professional endeavors.

1. Take online courses or enroll in professional development programs related to your field of interest. This will help you acquire new knowledge and skills.

2. Attend workshops, seminars, and conferences to gain insights from industry experts and network with professionals in your field.

3. Join professional organizations and associations to connect with like-minded individuals and stay updated on the latest industry trends and practices.

4. Seek mentorship or coaching from experienced professionals who can guide you and provide valuable feedback.

5. Engage in self-study by reading books, research papers, and articles related to your area of expertise. This will help broaden your knowledge base.

6. Practice regularly to develop and refine your skills. Whether it's through hands-on projects, simulations, or role-playing exercises, consistent practice is essential for improvement.

7. Collaborate with others on projects or join group activities where you can learn from your peers and exchange ideas.

8. Embrace challenges and step out of your comfort zone. Taking on tasks that push your limits will help you grow and develop new skills.

9. Seek feedback from colleagues, supervisors, or clients to identify areas for improvement and work on them.

10. Utilize online resources such as tutorials, video courses, and educational websites to learn new skills at your own pace.

11. Take advantage of on-the-job training opportunities or cross-functional projects that can expose you to different aspects of your organization or industry.

12. Develop a growth mindset by embracing a positive attitude towards learning, being open to feedback, and viewing failures as opportunities for improvement.

13. Stay updated on industry trends and technological advancements by following relevant blogs, podcasts, and social media accounts.

14. Volunteer for projects or initiatives that require skills you want to develop. This will provide practical experience and allow you to apply your knowledge in real-world scenarios.

15. Reflect on your experiences and learn from both successes and failures. This self-reflection will help you identify areas where you can improve and make better decisions in the future. Remember, continuous learning and skill development are lifelong pursuits. By actively seeking opportunities to expand your skill sets, you can stay competitive and adapt to the ever-changing demands of your profession.

Self-development is undeniably the cornerstone of personal wealth and growth. When one embarks on a journey of self-improvement, they open themselves up to a world of possibilities and opportunities. By dedicating time and effort to enhancing one's skills, knowledge, and mindset, individuals can unlock their full potential and achieve extraordinary success. However, the true value of self-development lies not only in personal gains but also in the ability to recognize and uplift others. As we immerse ourselves further into our own journey of growth, we become more attuned to the potential and worth in those around us. By offering guidance, support, and encouragement, we assist others in their pursuit of self-development, ultimately creating a ripple effect of positive transformation in both personal and professional spheres.

Educate Yourself on Money and Credit, Take Budgeting and Financial Classes

To achieve financial stability and make informed decisions regarding money and credit, it is imperative to prioritize self-education in these areas. By actively seeking out resources and knowledge, individuals can gain the necessary skills to navigate the complexities of personal finance. Taking budgeting and financial classes can provide invaluable insights into effective money management, enabling individuals to set realistic financial goals, create and adhere to budgets, and make informed decisions when it comes to credit and borrowing. Such classes offer a structured learning environment where participants can deepen their understanding of financial concepts, develop practical skills, and gain confidence in handling their personal finances. By investing in one's financial education, individuals can pave the way for a more secure and prosperous future. Here are a few options to get started.

1. Understanding the Basics: Start by educating yourself on the fundamentals of money and credit. Learn about the different types of accounts, credit scores, interest rates, and how they impact your financial health.

2. Read Books: There are numerous books available that can help you gain a deeper understanding of money management and credit. Some recommended titles include "The Total Money Makeover" by Dave Ramsey, "Rich Dad Poor Dad" by Robert Kiyosaki, and "I Will Teach You to Be Rich" by Ramit Sethi.

3. Online Courses: Take advantage of online platforms that offer budgeting and financial courses. Websites like Coursera, Udemy, and Khan Academy provide a wide range of free or affordable courses on personal finance, budgeting, and credit management.

4. Attend Workshops and Seminars: Many financial institutions, community organizations, and universities offer workshops and seminars on money management and credit. These events often provide valuable insights and practical tips for effectively managing your finances.

5. **Seek Professional Advice:** Consult with a financial advisor or credit counselor who can provide personalized guidance based on your specific financial situation. They can help you create a tailored budget, develop strategies to pay off debt, and offer advice on building credit.

6. **Stay Informed:** Keep up-to-date with the latest news and trends in finance and credit. Subscribe to reputable financial magazines, follow finance blogs, and listen to podcasts focused on money management and credit.

7. **Join Online Communities:** Engage with online communities and forums dedicated to personal finance and credit. These platforms provide opportunities to learn from others, ask questions, and share experiences and strategies for financial success.

8. **Use Financial Apps and Tools:** Utilize budgeting apps and financial tools to track your expenses, set financial goals, and monitor your credit score. Popular apps like Mint, YNAB (You Need a Budget), and Credit Karma can help you stay organized and make informed financial decisions.

9. **Network with Financial Professionals:** Attend networking events or join professional organizations

related to finance. Building connections with experts in the field can provide valuable insights and resources for improving your financial knowledge.

10. Continuously Educate Yourself: Money management and credit are dynamic areas, so it's essential to stay informed and continue learning. Stay curious, read articles, watch educational videos, and participate in webinars to continuously expand your financial literacy.

Remember, developing strong financial habits and becoming knowledgeable about money and credit is an ongoing process. By making a commitment

Utilize A Budget For Everything Everything Has A Budget

Operating within a budget has numerous benefits that can positively impact your financial health and overall well-being. Here are four key advantages of budgeting:

1. Financial Control: Budgeting helps you gain control over your money by allowing you to track and monitor your income and expenses. It enables you to allocate funds to different categories, prioritize your spending, and make informed decisions about where your money should go. By having a clear overview of your financial situation, you can avoid overspending, reduce debt, and achieve your financial goals.

2. Goal Setting and Achievement: A budget serves as a roadmap to achieving your financial goals. Whether you're saving for a down payment on a house, planning a vacation, or aiming to pay off your student loans,

budgeting helps you allocate funds towards these objectives. By setting realistic targets and tracking your progress, you can stay motivated and ensure you're on the right path to achieving your goals.

3. Improved Financial Awareness: Budgeting enhances your financial awareness by providing a comprehensive understanding of your income, expenses, and financial habits. It helps you identify areas where you may be overspending or where you can make adjustments to save money. This increased awareness allows you to make more informed financial decisions, avoid unnecessary expenses, and develop healthier financial habits.

4. Reduced Stress and Increased Peace of Mind: Operating with a budget can significantly reduce financial stress and bring peace of mind. When you have a clear plan for your money, you can avoid living paycheck to paycheck, manage unexpected expenses, and build an emergency fund. By knowing exactly where your money is going, you'll feel more in control and confident about your financial situation, leading to reduce stress and improved overall well-being.

WRITE A BUDGET FOR YOUR DREAMS

Creating a budget for your dreams is an essential step towards achieving your long-term aspirations. By meticulously planning and organizing your financial resources, you can effectively allocate funds towards the realization of your goals. Whether it's purchasing a new home, starting a business, or traveling the world, a well-structured budget acts as a roadmap to turn your dreams into tangible realities. It enables you to identify the necessary expenses, prioritize your spending, and make informed decisions regarding saving and investment strategies. A budget also promotes financial discipline, ensuring that you remain on track and avoid unnecessary debt or overspending.

With careful consideration and a proactive approach, a well-crafted budget empowers individuals to take control of their financial future and embark on a journey towards fulfilling their dreams.

INCLUDE EVERYTHING IN YOUR PERSONAL BUDGET

Start by including your fixed expenses, such as rent or mortgage payments, utilities, insurance premiums, and loan repayments. Next factor in variable expenses, such as groceries, transportation costs, entertainment, and dining out. Don't forget to account for irregular expenses like annual subscriptions, medical bills, and vehicle maintenance.

Additionally, allocate funds for savings, investments, and emergency funds to nurture a healthy financial future. Lastly, track discretionary spending to gain insight into areas where you can potentially cut back and redirect funds towards your financial goals. By diligently including all components of your personal budget, you can effectively manage your finances and achieve long-term financial stability.

INCLUDE VACATIONS IN YOUR BUDGET

Including vacations in your budget is a prudent and strategic move that can have numerous benefits for individuals and families alike. While vacations may be seen as a luxury expense, they can actually contribute to overall well-being and productivity. By allocating a portion of your budget towards vacations, you are prioritizing self-care and relaxation, which are essential for maintaining a healthy work-life balance. Additionally, taking regular vacations can have positive effects on mental health, reducing stress levels and increasing happiness. Furthermore, vacations provide an opportunity to explore new places, immerse oneself in different cultures, and create cherished memories with loved ones. By including vacations in your budget, you are not only investing in experiences and personal growth but also fostering stronger relationships with family and friends.

So, consider incorporating vacations into your financial planning to reap the long-term benefits they offer.

INCLUDE BIRTHDAYS IN YOUR BUDGET

Allocating a specific amount of money each month for birthdays, you can ensure that you have the necessary funds available to celebrate these special occasions without compromising your overall financial health. Whether it's for gifts, parties, or other birthday-related expenses, planning ahead and budgeting for birthdays allows you to thoughtfully allocate your resources and prioritize your spending. By incorporating birthdays into your budget, you can confidently and responsibly manage your finances while still enjoying the joyous celebrations that come with these memorable milestones.

Here is a step-by-step guide to help you draft your family budget.

1. Set financial goals: Determine what you want to achieve with your family budget. It could be saving for a vacation, paying off debts, or building an emergency fund. Having clear goals will help you align your budget accordingly.

2. Calculate your income: Gather all sources of income for your family, including salaries, investments, rental

income, and any other inflows. Make sure to consider both regular and irregular income sources.

3. Track your expenses: Review your bank statements, receipts, and bills from the past few months to get an accurate overview of your spending habits. Categorize expenses into different categories such as housing, utilities, groceries, transportation, entertainment, etc.

4. Identify areas for improvement: Analyze your expenses and look for areas where you can cut back or make adjustments. For example, consider reducing dining out expenses, finding cheaper alternatives for certain products or services, or negotiating better deals for utilities.

5. Create a budgeting template: Use spreadsheet software or budgeting apps to create a budget template that suits your needs. Include income sources, fixed expenses (e.g., mortgage, loan repayments), variable expenses (e.g., groceries, entertainment), and savings goals.

6. Allocate funds: Based on your income and expenses, allocate specific amounts to each category. Ensure that your income covers all your expenses and leaves room for savings. Remember to prioritize essential

expenses and savings before allocating funds for discretionary spending.

7. Involve all family members: Discuss and involve all family members in the budgeting process. Encourage open communication and collaboration to ensure everyone understands the financial goals and contributes to adhering to the budget.

8. Review and adjust regularly: Regularly review your budget to track your progress and make necessary adjustments. Expenses and income might change over time, so it's important to stay flexible and adapt your budget accordingly.

9. Save for emergencies and future goals: Allocate a portion of your budget towards an emergency fund to cover unexpected expenses. Additionally, set aside money for long-term goals like education, retirement, or purchasing a house.

10. Monitor and stay disciplined: Keep a close eye on your spending and regularly compare it against your budget. Stay disciplined and try to avoid unnecessary expenses that may derail your financial goals.

A family corporate budget is a tool to guide your financial decisions and help you achieve long term success.

SAVE MORE AND SPEND WISELY

This approach not only ensures financial stability but also cultivates a sense of responsibility and prudence. By meticulously examining our expenses, setting realistic budgets, and prioritizing our needs over wants, we can effectively curtail unnecessary expenditures and allocate our hard- earned income towards important financial goals, such as building an emergency fund or investing for the future. Moreover, saving more and spending wisely allows us to navigate unforeseen circumstances with ease, providing a safety net during challenging times. By exercising self-discipline and making informed financial decisions, we can attain long-term financial success and foster a secure and prosperous future. Embracing society's consumer mindsets come with significant troubles, with far-reaching consequences for individuals, their families, and their future prospects. Succumbing to the allure of consumerism often leads to a perpetual cycle of materialistic desires, which can result in financial strain, debt accumulation, and a lack of long-term financial security. It fosters a culture of instant gratification, where individuals prioritize immediate wants over essential needs and fail to cultivate a sense of financial discipline or responsibility. This mindset can also have adverse effects on personal relationships, as the pursuit of material possessions can overshadow the importance of genuine connections and emotional well-being. Moreover, a consumer-driven society tends to undervalue sustainability and environmental consciousness, further exacerbating the ecological challenges we face. Ultimately, succumbing to the consumer mindset jeopardizes one's ability to build a stable future, both personally and professionally, as it hinders the development of crucial skills such as financial literacy, critical thinking, and delayed gratification. Align your spending habits with a well-defined vision and budget. By letting your overarching goals and aspirations guide your financial decisions, you can ensure that every dollar spent contributes towards the realization of your family's dreams. A professional approach to spending involves creating a comprehensive budget that outlines your income, expenses, and savings targets. This budget should prioritize essential needs, while also allowing for prudent investments in education, health, and leisure activities that promote overall well-being. By maintaining a disciplined approach to spending, you can build a strong foundation for financial stability and create opportunities for your family's success.

Establish And Stay on Top of Your Credit Score

Individuals should be vigilant about monitoring their credit score in order to safeguard their financial well-being. A high credit score not only reflects responsible financial behavior, but also serves as a crucial determinant for accessing favorable interest rates and loan approvals. To stay on top of one's credit score, it is advisable to regularly review credit reports from reliable credit bureaus, promptly address any inaccuracies or discrepancies, and make timely payments towards outstanding debts. Additionally, keeping credit utilization below recommended thresholds and refraining from opening unnecessary lines of credit can positively impact one's creditworthiness. By adopting these proactive measures, individuals can proactively manage their credit score and pave the way towards a more secure financial future.

Establishing and maintaining a strong credit score is crucial for financial stability and success. By proactively managing your credit, you can ensure that you remain in control of your financial future. Here are some key strategies to help you establish and stay on top of your credit score:

1. Pay your bills on time: Timely payment of your credit card bills, loans, and other financial obligations is essential. Late payments can have a negative impact on your credit score, so make it a priority to pay your bills promptly.

2. Keep credit card balances low: It's important to maintain a low credit utilization ratio, which is the percentage of your available credit that you are currently using. Aim to keep your balances well below your credit limit to demonstrate responsible credit management.

3. Monitor your credit reports: Regularly reviewing your credit reports from the major credit bureaus (Equifax, Experian, and TransUnion) is crucial. Look for any errors or discrepancies that could be affecting your credit score and address them promptly.

4. Limit new credit applications: Be cautious when applying for new credit, as each application can result

in a hard inquiry on your credit report. Multiple inquiries within a short period of time can negatively impact your credit score. Only apply for new credit when absolutely necessary.

5. Diversify your credit mix: Having a healthy mix of credit accounts, such as credit cards, loans, and a mortgage, can positively influence your credit score. However, it's important to only take on credit that you can manage responsibly.

6. Avoid closing old credit accounts: Closing old credit accounts can shorten your credit history, which is an important factor in determining your credit score. If you have older accounts with a positive payment history, consider keeping them open to strengthen your credit profile.

7. Use credit monitoring tools: Take advantage of credit monitoring services that provide regular updates on changes to your credit report. These tools can help you detect any suspicious activity or potential identity theft.

8. By following these strategies, you can establish and maintain a strong credit score, which can open doors to better financial opportunities and provide you with greater peace of mind.

Purchase Real Estate

Investing in real estate has long been regarded as a prudent financial decision, providing families with a sense of security and the potential for substantial wealth accumulation. The purchase of real estate offers numerous benefits, both tangible and intangible, that contribute to a stable and prosperous future. Firstly, owning property provides a solid foundation for long-term financial security, as it serves as a valuable asset that appreciates over time. Additionally, real estate ownership allows families to build equity, which can be leveraged for future investments or used as collateral for loans. Moreover, the rental income generated from real estate investments can serve as a stable source of passive income, fostering financial independence and reducing reliance on traditional employment. Ultimately, the purchase of real estate not only offers a place to call home but also paves the way for a brighter and more prosperous future for families seeking financial stability.

Providing one's family with a home that is owned holds immense significance, not only from an emotional standpoint but also from a practical and strategic perspective. Owning a home establishes stability, security, and a sense of belonging for the family unit.

Here is a roadmap towards purchasing a Home for Your Family:

1. Determine your budget: Assess your financial situation and establish a realistic budget for your home purchase, considering your income, expenses, and savings.

2. Save for a down payment: Start saving for a down payment, aiming to have at least 20% of the home's purchase price. This will help you secure better loan terms and avoid private mortgage insurance (PMI).

3. Get pre-approved for a mortgage: Contact multiple lenders to get pre-approved for a mortgage. Compare interest rates, loan terms, and closing costs to find the best option for your needs. Pre-approval improves your bargaining power when making offers.

4. Hire a real estate agent: Find a reputable and experienced real estate agent who specializes in the

area you wish to buy a home. They will guide you through the process, help find suitable properties, negotiate offers, and handle paperwork.

5. Determine your needs and preferences: Make a list of the features and amenities you desire in a home, such as the number of bedrooms and bathrooms, size of the yard, location, proximity to schools, and accessibility to amenities.

6. Search for suitable properties: Utilize online listings, attend open houses, and work with your agent to find properties that meet your criteria. Visit potential homes and take notes to compare later.

7. Conduct a thorough inspection: Once you find a property you're interested in, hire a professional home inspector to assess its condition. A thorough inspection can uncover any hidden issues, ensuring you make an informed decision.

8. Review the neighborhood: Research the neighborhood thoroughly, considering factors like safety, schools, nearby amenities, and future development plans. Visit at different times of the day to get a sense of the area's atmosphere.

9. Make an offer: Work with your agent to determine a fair offer price based on comparable sales and market

conditions. Consider contingencies, such as appraisal and inspection, to protect yourself during the purchase process.

10. Negotiate and finalize the deal: Negotiate with the seller to reach an agreement on price, repairs, and other terms. Once a deal is reached, review and sign the purchase agreement, and provide the agreed-upon earnest money deposit.

11. Secure financing: Finalize your mortgage application with your chosen lender and provide all necessary documentation. Complete any additional requirements to secure your loan.

12. Get a home appraisal: The lender will arrange for an appraisal to determine the home's value and ensure

Establish Multiple Streams of Income

Establishing multiple streams of income is a wise financial strategy that can provide stability and security in an ever-changing economic landscape. Diversifying one's income sources not only mitigates the risks associated with relying on a single source, but it also allows individuals to maximize their earning potential. By exploring various avenues such as investments, entrepreneurship, freelancing, or passive income streams, individuals can create a robust financial portfolio that offers a consistent flow of income. This approach enables individuals to adapt to market fluctuations, seize new opportunities, and ultimately achieve financial independence. In today's competitive world, establishing multiple streams of income is a prudent and proactive step towards long-term financial success.

Checklist for Creating Streams of Income

1. Evaluate your talents and skill sets: Take some time to assess your strengths, interests, and skills. Identify the areas in which you excel and enjoy working.

2. Determine your niche: Based on your talents and skill sets, narrow down your focus to a specific niche or industry. This will help you position yourself as an expert in that particular field.

3. Research the market demand: Conduct thorough market research to determine the demand for your chosen niche. Explore the competition, identify potential clients, and understand the current trends and needs of the industry.

4. Build a portfolio: Create a portfolio showcasing your best work and projects related to your chosen niche. Include samples, case studies, testimonials, and any relevant experience that highlights your expertise.

5. Define your services: Clearly define the services you will offer as a freelancer. This could be writing, graphic design, web development, social media management, consulting, or any other field that aligns with your talents and skills.

6. Set you're pricing: Research industry standards and determine how much you will charge for your services. Consider factors such as your experience, the complexity of the projects, and the value you bring to clients.

7. Establish an online presence: Create a professional website or portfolio to showcase your work and attract potential clients. Utilize social media platforms and professional networking sites to connect with others in your industry and promote your services.

8. Develop a marketing strategy: Create a marketing plan to reach your target audience. This may include content marketing, social media advertising, attending industry events, or utilizing freelance platforms and job boards.

9. Network and collaborate: Attend industry events, workshops, and conferences to network with professionals in your field. Collaborate with other freelancers or agencies to expand your reach and gain new opportunities.

10. Create a business plan: Develop a comprehensive business plan that outlines your goals, target audience, pricing, marketing strategies, and financial

projections. This will help you stay focused and organized as you start your freelancing journey.

11. Establish legal and financial considerations: Register your freelance business, obtain any necessary licenses or permits, and consult with an accountant or financial advisor to ensure you are compliant with tax regulations and manage your finances effectively.

12. Secure your first clients: Reach out to potential clients, pitch your services, and leverage your network to secure your first freelance projects. Provide exceptional service and maintain professionalism to build a strong reputation and attract repeat business.

Hold Everyone Accountable For Their Own Financial Success

In the realm of financial stability and professional success, the fisherman mindset exudes a resolute commitment to holding others accountable. Just as a skilled angler patiently waits for the perfect moment to cast their line, the fisherman understands the importance of timing and strategy when encouraging individuals to take ownership of their financial well-being. With a calm and composed demeanor, the fisherman mindset acknowledges that personal responsibility lies at the heart of achieving prosperity. It champions the idea that every individual possesses the potential to navigate the currents of financial challenges and seize the opportunities that come their way. Just as a seasoned fisherman imparts knowledge and wisdom, this mindset seeks to empower others, fostering a culture of self-reliance and determination. It recognizes that by fostering accountability, individuals can chart their own course towards financial stability and professional success.

While lending money and enabling others may seem like acts of kindness or support, there are several reasons why it can be considered wrong and problematic. **Here are a few:**

1. Dependency: When you lend money or enable someone, it can create a dependency on you or the financial support you provide. This can lead to a cycle of dependence, where the person never learns to manage their own finances or take responsibility for their actions.

2. Lack of accountability: By constantly lending money or enabling others, you may inadvertently prevent them from facing the consequences of their actions. This can hinder personal growth, as individuals may not learn from their mistakes if they are always bailed out.

3. Financial strain: Constantly lending money or enabling others can put a significant financial strain on your own life. It can lead to a situation where you are constantly sacrificing your own financial stability to support someone else, potentially putting your own future at risk.

4. Strained relationships: Money matters can often strain relationships, especially when there are

expectations or tensions related to lending. If the borrower fails to repay or misuses the funds, it can lead to resentment, anger, or damaged trust between you and the borrower.

5. Encouraging bad habits: Enabling others by lending money can inadvertently enable negative behaviors or habits. If the person is using the money for unhealthy or destructive activities, such as substance abuse, it may indirectly contribute to their harm rather than helping them.

6. Unequal power dynamics: When one person consistently lends money or enables others, it can create an imbalance of power in the relationship. The borrower may feel obligated to comply with the lender's wishes or decisions, leading to a loss of autonomy and potential exploitation.

7. Financial education: By constantly providing financial support, you may inadvertently hinder the person's ability to learn financial responsibility and independence. It is important for individuals to develop their own financial management skills and learn from their own experiences.

While lending money and enabling others can be well-intentioned, it is crucial to consider the potential negative consequences and long-term impact on both parties involved. It is essential to encourage personal growth, accountability, and financial independence rather than fostering dependency and perpetuating unhealthy habits.

Here are some polite and assertive ways to say no when someone asks for money or a handout, while encouraging personal responsibility and accountability:

1. I'm sorry, but I'm not able to give you money. However, I can offer advice on finding local resources that might be able to assist you.

2. I understand your situation, but I believe in empowering individuals to find their own solutions. Have you considered exploring job opportunities or reaching out to community organizations for support?

3. I'm unable to provide financial assistance, but I'd be happy to help you brainstorm alternative ways to address your current needs.

4. I'm practicing personal financial responsibility at the moment, so I'm unable to give you money. However, there might be other ways I can support you, such as sharing information about local job fairs or vocational training programs.

5. I'm sorry, but I'm not in a position to give money. I believe it's important for individuals to take proactive steps towards improving their

6. circumstances. Is there anything else I can do to support you?"

7. I'm sorry to hear about your situation, but I'm not able to provide financial assistance. However, I encourage you to connect with social service agencies in our area that specialize in helping individuals facing similar challenges."

8. I'm currently focusing on my own financial goals and commitments, so I'm unable to give you money. Let's explore other options together, like finding local organizations that provide job training or assistance with housing."

9. I understand that you're going through a tough time, but I believe in encouraging personal responsibility. Instead of giving money, I can offer guidance on budgeting or connecting with employment services.

10. I'm sorry, but I'm not comfortable giving money. However, I'd be more than willing to help you research local resources that can provide the support you need.

11. I'm unable to provide financial assistance, as I believe in fostering self-sufficiency. Have you considered seeking out educational opportunities or programs that can help you develop new skills? It is important to express empathy and offer alternative forms of support while maintaining your boundaries.

BONUS:

Build Wealth for The Long Term

Achieving success in money management may seem like an arduous undertaking, and indeed, it demands considerable effort. However, it is imperative to acknowledge that the pursuit of financial proficiency necessitates a diligent and dedicated approach. The intricacies of effectively managing one's finances demand careful attention to detail, comprehensive planning, and a thorough understanding of various economic factors. It is essential to recognize that the rewards of such endeavors far outweigh the initial investment of time and energy. By adopting a professional mindset and embracing the challenges that come with it, individuals can pave their path towards financial success, ensuring a secure and prosperous future.

In order to achieve sustained success and fulfillment, adopting a mindset that encompasses long-term vision and strategic planning is paramount. By thinking on and building our lives for the long haul, we can position ourselves for enduring growth and prosperity. This involves setting clear goals and objectives that align with our values and aspirations, and then meticulously charting a path towards their realization. It requires careful consideration of the potential challenges and obstacles that may arise along the way and developing contingency plans to overcome them. By cultivating a professional mindset that emphasizes foresight and perseverance, we can navigate the complexities of life with confidence and resilience, ensuring that our efforts yield lasting and meaningful outcomes.

In the realm of financial discourse, wealth is often equated solely with monetary assets and material possessions. However, adopting a comprehensive perspective reveals that wealth encompasses a far broader scope than mere financial abundance. True wealth encompasses an amalgamation of various components, such as physical and mental well- being, harmonious relationships, personal development, and a sense of purpose. Acknowledging the multidimensionality of wealth is crucial in cultivating a holistic understanding that extends beyond material wealth, thus enabling individuals to pursue a more fulfilling and balanced existence. In essence, wealth transcends the boundaries of monetary value and encompasses the richness derived from various facets of life.

Success is not truly success if we neglect our homes and focus solely on our own achievements. Wealth and prosperity go far beyond material possessions and professional accolades; they reside within the warmth and love of our families. Our homes are the foundation upon which our dreams are built, and it is within the walls of our abode that true wealth is found. It is in the laughter and shared moments around the dinner table, the support and comfort during difficult times, and the joy of watching our loved ones grow and thrive.

Longevity in success is not measured by individual triumphs alone, but by the harmonious balance we achieve within our homes, nurturing our families with love and kindness.

By incorporating the insightful principles outlined in this book and implementing them into your daily life, you have the potential to attain not only financial prosperity, but also establish yourself as a person of significance, capable of exerting a substantial influence within your household, community, and the wider world. As a result, you will acquire substantial wealth.

Money

These verses inspire us to approach our financial lives with wisdom and integrity.

Proverbs 22:7: "The rich rule over the poor, and the borrower is slave to the lender."

This verse reminds us of the importance of managing our finances wisely, avoiding excessive debt, and striving for financial freedom.

Matthew 6:19-21: "Do not store up for yourselves treasures on earth, where moths and vermin destroy, and where thieves break in and steal. But store up for yourselves treasures in heaven, where moths and vermin do not destroy, and where thieves do not break in and steal. For where your treasure is, there your heart will be also.

These powerful words encourage us to prioritize eternal treasures over temporary wealth, emphasizing the significance of generosity and investing in matters of eternal value.

Luke 16:10: "Whoever can be trusted with very little can also be trusted with much, and whoever is dishonest with very little will also be dishonest with much."

This verse reminds us that how we handle small amounts of money reflects our character and ability to handle greater resources. It encourages us to be trustworthy stewards, no matter the size of our financial blessings.

Proverbs 11:24-25: "One person gives freely, yet gains even more; another withholds unduly, but comes to poverty. A generous person will prosper; whoever refreshes others will be refreshed."

This verse emphasizes the power of generosity, teaching us that when we open our hearts and hands to bless others, we ourselves are enriched beyond measure. It reminds us that true wealth lies in acts of kindness and selflessness.

Malachi 3:10: Bring the whole tithe into the storehouse, that there may be food in my house. Test me in this," says the Lord Almighty, "and see if I will not throw open the floodgates of heaven and pour out so much blessing that there will not be room enough to store it.

This verse encourages us to honor God with our finances by faithfully tithing and giving back to His work. It assures us that when we trust God in our giving, He will abundantly bless us in return.

Prudent: Budget

Proverbs 12:23 - "A prudent man conceals knowledge, but the heart of fools proclaims folly."

Proverbs 14:15 - "The simple believes everything, but the prudent gives thought to his steps."

Proverbs 22:3 - "The prudent sees danger and hides himself, but the simple go on and suffers for it."

Matthew 10:16 - "Behold, I am sending you out as sheep in the midst of wolves, so be wise as serpents and innocent as doves."

Luke 14:28 - "For which of you, desiring to build a tower, does not first sit down and count the cost, whether he has enough to complete it?"

Ephesians 5:15-16 - "Look carefully then how you walk, not as unwise but as wise, making the best use of the time because the days are evil."

Colossians 4:5 - "Walk in wisdom toward outsiders, making the best use of the time."

James 1:5 - "If any of you lacks wisdom, let him ask God, who gives generously to all without reproach, and it will be given him."

Multiple streams of income

Proverbs 31:16 - "She considers a field and buys it; with the fruit of her hands she plants a vineyard." This verse highlights the importance of investing and diversifying one's income sources.

Ecclesiastes 11:2 - "Give a portion to seven, or even to eight, for you know not what disaster may happen on earth." This verse encourages us to distribute our resources wisely, indicating the significance of having multiple streams of income as a safeguard against unforeseen circumstances.

Proverbs 10:4 - "A slack hand causes poverty, but the hand of the diligent makes rich." By emphasizing the importance of hard work and diligence, this verse implies that seeking multiple avenues for income can lead to prosperity.

Luke 16:10 - "One who is faithful in a very little is also faithful in much, and one who is dishonest in a very little is also dishonest in much." This scripture reminds us that being faithful and responsible with small opportunities can open doors to larger ones, including the pursuit of multiple streams of income.

Proverbs 13:11 - earth gained hastily will dwindle, but whoever gathers little by little will increase it." This verse advises against seeking quick riches, instead emphasizing the value of steady, incremental progress towards financial stability through diverse income sources.

1 Timothy 5:8 - But if anyone does not provide for his relatives, and especially for members of his household, he has denied the faith and is worse than an unbeliever." This scripture underscores the importance of providing for our

families and loved ones, suggesting that having multiple streams of income can help fulfill this responsibility.

Proverbs 14:23 - "In all toil there is profit, but mere talk tends only to poverty." By promoting diligent work and action, this verse suggests that actively pursuing various income streams is more fruitful than merely talking about potential opportunities.

Abraham:

Abraham resided in the land of Canaan, where he held a prominent position as a prosperous and esteemed individual, renowned for his wisdom and benevolence. Through his extensive livestock and possessions, Abraham had amassed significant wealth, and his nephew Lot resided with him. Following the passing of Lot's father, Abraham's brother Haran, Abraham assumed the role of a father figure for Lot. However, after spending a considerable amount of time together, Abraham recognized the necessity of allowing Lot to forge his own path in life. Abraham comprehended the significance of stewardship as mandated by God. It is our duty to nurture and cultivate those whom God has entrusted to our care, and when the divinely appointed time arrives, to release them as adults so they may embark on their own journey to fulfill their purpose on Earth.

Lot, a young and ambitious man, had also prospered under Abraham's guidance. He had grown fond of the fertile plains of Jordan and desired to settle there with his own people and livestock. Recognizing Lot's aspirations, Abraham approached him one day and said, "Lot, my nephew, we have been blessed abundantly, and our flocks have multiplied. It is time for us to part ways and establishes our own lives.

Lot, though grateful for Abraham's guidance, was hesitant to leave his uncle's side. He had grown accustomed to the comfort and security of Abraham's wealth. However, Abraham assured him that it was time for them to separate, allowing each of them to mature and manage their own lives.

With a heavy heart, Lot agreed to part ways with his beloved uncle. They decided to divide the land between them, with Abraham giving Lot the first choice. Lot's eyes gleamed with excitement as he surveyed the lush plains of Jordan, filled with abundant water and fertile soil. Without hesitation, he chose the Jordan Valley as his new home.

Abraham, on the other hand, settled in the land of Canaan, a place that would later become known as the Promised Land. Though not as fertile as the Jordan Valley, Abraham trusted in God's providence and believed that his faithfulness would be rewarded.

As time passed, Lot's decision to settle in the Jordan Valley proved to be both a blessing and a curse. The land was indeed fertile, and his flocks multiplied rapidly. However, the inhabitants of the nearby cities, Sodom and Gomorrah, were wicked and corrupt. Lot found himself surrounded by immorality and temptation, which began to erode his own moral compass.

Meanwhile, Abraham continued to prosper in the land of Canaan. God blessed him with even greater wealth, and his reputation as a wise and just man spread far and wide. He became a respected leader among his people, and his faith in God remained unshakable.

One fateful day, disaster struck the cities of Sodom and Gomorrah. God, in His righteous judgment, decided to destroy the wickedness that had consumed the land. Abraham, being a man of compassion, pleaded with God to spare the cities if even a few righteous people could be found. God agreed, and Abraham's nephew, Lot, was among those who were saved.

Lot's wife died when leaving Sodom and Gomorrah due to not following the complete instructions of God that had been given to her. Lot having witnessed the destruction of his family and the consequences of his choices, realized the importance of stewardship and the need to align his life with God's will.

True wealth is not found in the accumulation of material possessions, but rather, it resides in leading a life that is firmly rooted in God. It is aligning our actions with the teachings and guidance bestowed upon us by God, while responsibly managing the blessings entrusted to us.

Joshua:

In the ancient land of Canaan, a great leader named Joshua emerged to guide the people of Israel into the Promised Land. Joshua was a man of unwavering faith, chosen by God to fulfill a divine purpose. With the passing of Moses, Joshua stepped forward, ready to lead the Israelites to the land flowing with milk and honey.

As Joshua stood on the banks of the Jordan River, he could feel the weight of responsibility on his shoulders. The land before him was filled with lush greenery, fertile soil, and abundant resources. It was a land promised to the descendants of Abraham, Isaac, and Jacob, a land where they could establish their own nation and worship their God freely.

With the Ark of the Covenant leading the way, Joshua commanded the people to prepare themselves for the journey ahead. They crossed the Jordan River on dry ground, just as their ancestors had crossed the Red Sea. This miraculous event served as a reminder that God was with them, guiding their every step.

As they entered the land, Joshua faced numerous challenges. The Canaanites, Amorites, and other tribes inhabited the land, fiercely guarding their territories. But Joshua remained steadfast, trusting in God's promises. He led the Israelites in battle, conquering city after city, as God granted them victory.

The walls of Jericho crumbled at the sound of the Israelites' trumpets, and the city was taken. The sun stood still in the sky, allowing Joshua and his army to defeat their enemies. With each victory, the Israelites grew stronger, and the land of Canaan slowly became their own.

Joshua divided the land among the twelve tribes of Israel, ensuring that each tribe received their rightful inheritance. He was meticulous in his distribution, ensuring fairness and justice for all. The land was rich with resources, and the people flourished under Joshua's wise leadership.

But Joshua's true wealth did not lie in the land or possessions. His true wealth was the faith and trust he had in God. He knew that it was God who had led them to this land, and it was God who had given them victory. Joshua's heart was filled with gratitude, and he constantly sought God's guidance in all his decisions.

Under Joshua's leadership, the Israelites lived in peace and prosperity for many years. They worshipped their God, followed His commandments, and enjoyed the blessings of the Promised Land. Joshua's legacy as a faithful leader and a man of God was etched into the hearts of the people, and his story continues to inspire generations to come.

In the end, Joshua's wealth was not measured by material possessions, but by the love and devotion he had for his people and his unwavering faith in God. He had fulfilled his purpose, leading the Israelites into the land of promise, and his name would forever be remembered as a symbol of courage, faith, and the fulfillment of God's promises.

King David

Once upon a time, in the ancient land of Israel, there lived a young shepherd boy named David. He was known for his unwavering faith in God and his exceptional musical talent. David possessed a unique gift for playing the harp, and his melodies had the power to soothe even the most troubled souls.

David's story began when he was chosen by the prophet Samuel to be anointed as the future king of Israel. At that time, the current king, Saul, was plagued by an evil spirit, and David's music was the only thing that could bring him solace.

David's harp-playing not only brought comfort to Saul but also caught the attention of the entire kingdom.

As David grew older, his reputation as a skilled musician spread far and wide. People from all walks of life would gather to hear him play, and his music became a symbol of

hope and inspiration. David's melodies were not merely a form of entertainment; they were a way for him to express his deep love and devotion to God.

One day, as David was tending to his flock in the fields, he received a message from the prophet Nathan. God had chosen David to be the next king of Israel, and his reign would be marked by great wealth and prosperity. David was both humbled and excited by this news, but he knew that his true wealth lay in his faithfulness to God.

When David finally ascended to the throne, he ruled with wisdom and integrity. He used his newfound wealth to improve the lives of his people, ensuring that no one in his kingdom went hungry or lacked shelter. David's generosity knew no bounds, and he made it his mission to uplift the less fortunate.

Despite his wealth and power, David never forgot his humble beginnings as a shepherd boy. He continued to play his harp, not only in the grand halls of his palace but also in the quiet corners of his kingdom. David's music became a symbol of his unwavering faith and a reminder to his people of the importance of worshiping God.

Throughout his reign, David faced numerous challenges and trials, but he never wavered in his faith. He relied on his gifts, both musical and spiritual, to guide him through the darkest of times. David's faithfulness and devotion to God were the pillars upon which his kingdom stood.

In the end, David's reign was marked by prosperity, peace, and the enduring legacy of his faith. His story became a testament to the power of using one's gifts to worship God and serve others. David's wealth was not measured in material possessions but in the love and respect he earned from his people.

And so, the biblical account of King David reminds us that true wealth lies not in the accumulation of riches but in the faithful use of our gifts to honor God and uplift those around us.

King Solomon

Once upon a time, in the ancient land of Israel, there lived a wise and prosperous king named Solomon. He was the son of King David, a man after God's own heart. From a young age, Solomon had been blessed with extraordinary wisdom, a gift bestowed upon him by the Almighty.

As Solomon ascended to the throne, he sought to honor God and lead his people with justice and righteousness. One night, as he lay in deep slumber, God appeared to him in a dream and said, Ask for whatever you want me to give you.

Solomon, recognizing the magnitude of this opportunity, humbly replied, "Lord, you have shown great kindness to my father David, and you have made me king in his place. But I am young and inexperienced. Give me wisdom and knowledge, that I may govern your people with discernment and understanding.

Pleased with Solomon's request, God granted him not only wisdom but also riches and honor beyond measure. The news of Solomon's wisdom spread far and wide, attracting the attention of neighboring kingdoms and even distant lands. Kings and queens from all corners of the earth journeyed to witness the splendor of Solomon's court and to seek his counsel.

Solomon's wealth was unparalleled. His kingdom flourished, and silver and gold became as common as stones in the streets of Jerusalem. The people marveled at the grandeur of his palace, adorned with precious jewels and exquisite craftsmanship. Yet, despite his opulence, Solomon remained humble, never forgetting that his blessings were a result of God's grace.

One day, two women approached Solomon, both claiming to be the mother of a newborn baby. Unable to determine the true mother, Solomon devised a plan to test their love and compassion. He ordered a sword to be brought and declared, "Cut the living child in two and give half to one and half to the other.

One woman, driven by her maternal instincts, cried out, Please, my lord, give her the living baby! Do not kill him! Solomon, with his divine wisdom, discerned the true mother and said, "Give the baby to the first woman, for she is the real mother. She would rather give up her child than see him harmed."

News of this wise judgment spread throughout the land, solidifying Solomon's reputation as a just and fair ruler. People from all walks of life sought his counsel, bringing him their most complex disputes and dilemmas. Solomon's wisdom became a beacon of hope, guiding his people through the darkest of times.

But amidst all his wealth and wisdom, Solomon never lost sight of his faith in God. He built a magnificent temple in Jerusalem, a place of worship and reverence for the Almighty. He offered sacrifices and prayers, seeking guidance and strength to fulfill his duties as king.

As the years passed, Solomon's wisdom and wealth continued to grow, and his reign became known as the golden age of Israel. His legacy as a wise and faithful king endured for generations, inspiring leaders to seek wisdom and trust in God.

The biblical account of King Solomon serves as a reminder that true wealth lies not in material possessions but in the wisdom and faith we possess. It teaches us that when we seek God's guidance and trust in His providence, we can overcome any challenge and lead with righteousness and compassion.

The end

Scripture encourages us to build our lives upon solid precepts, for they are the foundation of wisdom and success.

Proverbs 24:3-4 - "By wisdom a house is built, and through understanding it is established; through knowledge its rooms are filled with rare and beautiful treasures." These verses remind us that wisdom and understanding are the building blocks of a well-founded life.

Luke 6:48 - "He is like a man building a house, who dug down deep and laid the foundation on rock. When a flood came, the torrent struck that house but could not shake it because it was well built." This passage emphasizes the importance of constructing our lives on a solid foundation, symbolizing the unwavering principles that withstand any storms that may come our way.

Matthew 7:24-25 - "Therefore everyone who hears these words of mine and puts them into practice is like a wise man who built his house on the rock. The rain came down, the streams rose, and the winds blew and beat against that house; yet it did not fall because it had its foundation on the rock." Here, Jesus teaches us that true wisdom lies in not only hearing but also applying His teachings in our daily lives.

Psalm 127:1 - "Unless the Lord builds the house, the builder's labor in vain. Unless the Lord watches over the city, the guards stand watch in vain." This verse serves as a poignant reminder that without the guidance and presence of the Lord, our efforts to build a meaningful life will be in vain.

Ephesians 2:20 - "Built on the foundation of the apostles and prophets, with Christ Jesus himself as the chief cornerstone." This scripture highlights the significance of Jesus as the cornerstone of our lives, and how His teachings, along with those of the apostles and prophets, form the solid foundation upon which we should build.

Proverbs 14:1 - "The wise woman builds her house, but with her own hands the foolish one tears hers down." This verse speaks to the importance of wise decision-making and the impact it has on our lives. By building upon precepts, we create a firm foundation that promotes growth and success.

May this book inspire us to construct our lives upon the strong precepts of wisdom and understanding through building upon these principles, we can withstand any challenges and create lives that are truly impactful.

www.ingramcontent.com/pod-product-compliance
Lightning Source LLC
Chambersburg PA
CBHW051133160426
43195CB00014B/2461